Drew Launay

Oval Books

Published by Oval Books
335 Kennington Road
London SE11 4QE
United Kingdom

Telephone: +44 (0)20 7582 7123
Fax: +44 (0)20 7582 1022
E-mail: info@ovalbooks.com
Web site: www.ovalbooks.com

Language Consultants – Stefan Zeidenitz,
   Alda Guderian-Stein and Michael Moore

Illustrator – Charles Hemming

Series Editor – Anne Tauté

Cover Designers – Jim Wire and Vicki Towers
Printer – Gopsons Papers Ltd.
Producer – Oval Projects Ltd.

Xenophobe's® is a Registered Trademark.

The Xenophobe's® Guide to The Germans
makes the perfect companion to this
Xenophobe's® Lingo Learner.

ISBN-13: 978-1-903096-15-4
ISBN-10: 1-903096-15-4

Contents

Introduction

When abroad you have to expect foreigners. Most of these foreigners will not speak English. Worse, to them, you are the foreigner. This book is to help you overcome such a setback and cope with the need to communicate with the natives. Phrases are given in English. Then in German in *italics*. Then the pronunciation is set out for the English tongue in **bold** type.

Speedy speech can make all the difference. The faster and more deliberately you say the bits in bold, the more you will convince the natives that what they are hearing is their own language.

Pronunciation

The most common sound in German is that which comes from the back of the throat when clearing out mucous. In German it is written as 'ch' and sounds pretty much like the end of the Scottish word "loch". Practise, at a safe distance from your friends, with the German word for eight: *acht* (**uch-t**). To help you, this sound has been placed in small capital letters CH whenever it occurs, e.g: **uCHt**. It has to be pointed out that in some regions this sound is pronounced 'ish', but to remain sane it's better not to think about regional accents.

German enunciation tends to be guttural and brutal, so bear this in mind when you attempt the following special sounds:

a should be uttered as a dissatisfied '**uh**', as in '**bunk**'.

au as in the word '*blau*' (blue) is pronounced '**ow!**' as in 'That really hurt' not '**oh**' as in 'Oh dear', so where it occurs, the sound will be given an **!** to remind you.

b within a word is pronounced like '**p**' (but not always).

d is pronounced like 't', as in *'hund'* (**hoont**), hound.

e at the end of a word should sound like 'er'.

e can also be pronounced 'ay'. This explains why many sentences in German seem to contain the word 'gay'. For example: *gehen* (**gay en**) which means go; and *Geflügelinnereien* (**Gay flew girl in orion**) which means giblets.

ei is pronounced **eye**, as in *drei*, three.

g is hard as in 'gun', e.g., *'Guten abend'* (**Goo ten are bent**) – Good afternoon.

j is pronounced 'y', as in 'yuk'.

ö is pronounced 'ur', as in 'urn'.

s is sometimes pronounced like 'z', as in zoom; sometimes like 'sh', and sometimes as just plain 's'.

ß (the speedy sign for double 's') as in *Straße* (**Strah sir**), street.

Sch should be hissed abruptly like 'shh', as in 'shut up'.

ü is pronounced 'ue' as in 'due'.

v is an 'f', e.g., *'volk'* which is pronounced **folk** and means folk, or *verboten* (**fair boat ten**) which means forbidden.

w is like 'v' as in *'wagen'* (**vah gun**), wagon. Hence *Volkswagen* is pronounced **Folks vah gun**.

z is like 'ts', as in 'tse-tse fly'.

To overcome all these basic problems, this book opts for the easiest way out which is to go for as credible an approximation as possible. Thus, in a sentence such as:

Wo ist die Generalstaatsverordnetenversammlung?

When is the meeting of the legislature?

everybody will understand you if you say it like this:

Vo / ist / dee / Gainer rahl shh tarts fair ord net ten fair zum loong?

Aside from the pronounciation, you will have noted the one rather long word in the sentence. This is very common in German and should be accepted philosophically and perhaps with reading glasses.

Of course, you could forget trying to sound German and go for sounding like someone who normally speaks English. This will not only simplify matters for you but may encourage the Germans to forgive your lack of effort, though this is doubtful.

The Alphabet   *Das Alphabet* Duss / Alfa bait

Sticklers for law and order, it is likely that a German authority will, sooner or later, ask you to prove your identity by spelling out your name. For this you should know the sounds of individual letters. It is quite useful, also, for ordering a take-away.

A **ah**	H **har**	O **oh**	U **ooh**
B **beh**	I **ee**	P **peh**	V **fow!**
C **seh**	J **yacht**	Q **koo**	W **veh**
D **deh**	K **car**	R **air**	X **icks**
E **eh**	L **ell**	S **ess**	Y **ipp see lon**
F **eff**	M **em**	T **teh**	Z **tss set**
G **geh**	N **en**		

Avoid Grammar Like the Plague

Unless you are an intellectual masochist, you should avoid thinking about the construction of the German language. There are a great many rules, let alone the complications of nominatives, genitives, accusatives, indicatives, imperatives, obligatives, perfects, imperfects and pluperfects, which are hazardous to mental health.

Even genders are a law unto themselves. A girl is sexless (being not a 'she' but an 'it'), a turnip is female, some parts of the body are male, others female, and yet others are neuter. So the best thing is to be armed with the following short phrase if reprimanded for lack of attention to detail when asking your way home where you might want to be after a very short time:

Excuse me.
Entschuldigung.
Ent shool dee goong.

There are two other forms of apology:

I am sorry.
Es tut mir Leid.
Es toot mere Light.

Forgive me.
Verzeihen Sie.
Fairts eye en / Zee.

Relief, however, can be found in one firm rule which you may already have noticed. All nouns start with a capital letter wherever they happen to be in a sentence – so they can easily be spotted among the other grammatical hazards.

Possible Pitfalls

After does not mean 'that which follows', but 'anus' or 'backside' which, in a way, follows.

Bad does not mean 'rotten' but 'bath' or 'spa' which the Germans are very fond of.

Fahrt (pronounced 'fart') means a journey. *Einfahrt* means entry, and *Ausfahrt* (**ow!ss fart**) means exit. Also *Einfahrt* and *Ausfahrt* only refer to traffic. When people (not vehicles) are entering or exiting a place the terms used are *Eingang* and *Ausgang*. On the other hand, an actual fart is *Pup* pronounced 'poop'.

Gift does not mean a present, but 'poison'.
hell does not mean 'down under' but 'clear and bright'.
damit is not an expletive, but means 'with that'.
dick means thick, large, bulky, big.

5

Essential Words to Remember

Very nearly everything can be mimed. You can nod your head for "yes". Shake your head for "no". You can hold up fingers for numbers, and point rudely at anything you wish to indicate. You cannot, however, mime colours, the past, the present or the future.

If you lost a silver laptop in a concert hall yesterday, you can convey lost by looking desperate, laptop by dancing your fingers on your knees for a few seconds, concert hall by waving an imaginary baton and humming Wagner's *Lohengrin*, but 'silver' and 'yesterday' are tricky. The following should therefore be kept handy:

Black	*schwarz*	**shh varts**
White	*weiß*	**vice**
Red	*rot*	**rot**
Orange	*orange*	**oh ranch**
Yellow	*gelb*	**gelp**
Green	*grün*	**groon**
Blue	*blau*	**blow!** (not 'oh' but 'ow!')
Violet	*violett*	**vee oh let**
Brown	*braun*	**brown**
Silver	*silber*	**zil ber**
Yesterday	*gestern*	**guess stairn**
Today	*heute*	**hoiter**
Tomorrow	*morgen*	**more gun**

That is not my mine.
Das ist nicht meins.
Duss / ist / niCHt / mines.

However, the most essential word to remember, with which you should always end every question if you wish to survive is:

Please   *Bitte*   **Bitter**

Once you have received an answer you should mumble a humble:

Thank you.
Danke schön.
Dunker / shurn. Or even:

Thank you very much.
Vielen Dank.
Feelin / Dunk.

Less Essential But Jolly Useful Words and Phrases

Yes	*ja*	**yar**
No	*nein*	**nine**
Hello	*Hallo*	**Hull law**
Goodbye	*Auf Wiedersehen*	**Ow!f / Vee dare zane**
Good morning	*Guten Morgen*	**Goo en / More gun**
Good afternoon	*Guten Tag*	**Goo ten / Tug**
Good evening	*Guten Abend*	**Goo ten / Are bent**
Good night	*Gute Nacht*	**Goo ter / NahCHt**

I beg your pardon.
Wie bitte?
Vee / bitter?

Toilets (always an embarrassing one to mime)
Toiletten
Toilet ten

Sod off.
Hau ab.
How! / up.

The Family   *Die Familie*   Dee / Fam meal yer

You may be frog-marched to meet the family and this will demand, at the very least, an attempt at understanding who is who:

Mother	*Mutter*	**Mooter**
Father	*Vater*	**Farter**
Daughter	*Tochter*	**Toch ter**
Son	*Sohn*	**Zone**
Wife	*Ehefrau*	**Ay er frow!**
Husband	*Ehemann*	**Ay er mun**
Sister	*Schwester*	**Shh vester**
Brother	*Bruder*	**Brooder**
Grandmother	*Großmutter*	**Grows mooter**
Grandfather	*Großvater*	**Grows farter**
Aunt	*Tante*	**Tunter**
Uncle	*Onkel*	**Ong kell**
Cousin	*Cousin*	**Coo zan**
Niece	*Nichte*	**Nich ter**
Nephew	*Neffe*	**Nef fur**
Mother-in-law	*Schwiegermutter*	**Shh veeger mooter**
Father-in-law	*Schwiegervater*	**Shh veeger farter**

How do you do?
Wie geht es Ihnen?
Vee / gate / ess / Eee nun.

Pleased to meet you.
Erfreut, Sie kennenzulernen, sehr erfreut.
Air froit, / Zee / ken ent zoo learnen, / zair / air froit.

Why does your mother look at me that way?
Warum schaut deine Mutter mich so an?
Vah rum / shout / dine er / Mooter / mich / zo / an?

8

Small Talk

German humour does not easily run to whimsy – which is likely to be taken seriously, with dire consequences. Any attempt at irony such as 'Nice weather for ducks!' or 'What a lovely day!' when it's pouring with rain will leave them confused, to which they will quickly adjust by deciding that you are unfortunately loopy. It is therefore always best to state the obvious:

It's very wet today.
Es ist sehr nass heute.
Ess / ist / zair / nass / hoiter.

It's a bit cold.
Es ist ein bisschen kalt.
Ess / ist / ine / bish on / cult.

It's freezing.
Es ist Frost.
Ess / ist / Frost.

Numerals *Ziffern* Tss siff fan

One	*eins/eine/ein*	**eye ens** or **eye ner** or **ine**
Two	*zwei*	**tss veye**
Three	*drei*	**dry**
Four	*vier*	**fear**
Five	*fünf*	**foonf**
Six	*sechs*	**zeCHs**
Seven	*sieben*	**zee ben**
Eight	*acht*	**ahCHt**
Nine	*neun*	**noin**
Ten	*zehn*	**tss sane**
Eleven	*elf*	**elf**

Twelve	*zwölf*	**tss velf**
Thirteen	*dreizehn*	**dry tss en**
Fourteen	*vierzehn*	**fear tss en**
Fifteen	*fünfzehn*	**foonf tss en**
Sixteen	*sechzehn*	**zeCH tss en**
Seventeen	*siebzehn*	**zeep tss en**
Eighteen	*achtzehn*	**ahCHt tss en**
Nineteen	*neunzehn*	**noin tss en**

Twenty	*zwanzig*	**tss vunt sig**
Twenty one	*einundzwanzig*	**eye noon tss vunt sig**
Twenty two	*zweiundzwanzig*	**tss veye oon tss vunt sig**
Twenty three	*dreiundzwanzig*	**dry oon tss vunt sig** etc.

Thirty	*dreißig*	**dry sig**
Forty	*vierzig*	**fear tsig**
Fifty	*fünfzig*	**foonf tsig**
Sixty	*sechzig*	**zeCH tsig**
Seventy	*siebzig*	**zeep tsig**
Eighty	*achtzig*	**ahCH tsig**
Ninety	*neunzig*	**noin tsig**

One Hundred	*hundert*	**hoon dirt**
Two hundred	*zweihundert*	**tss veye hoon dirt**
Three hundred	*dreihundert*	**dry hoon dirt** etc.

One thousand	*eintausend*	**ine tow!s sent**
Two thousand	*zweitausend*	**tss veye tow!s sent**
Three thousand	*dreitausend*	**dry tow!s sent** etc.

One hundred thousand *hundert tausend* **hoon dirt ow!s sent**

| First | *erstens* | **airs tense** |
| Second | *zweitens* | **tss veye tense** |

| Quarter | *Viertel* | **Fear tell** |
| Half | *Hälfte* | **Hellf ter** |

Days of the Week   *Wochentage*   VOCH en tugger

Monday	*Montag*	**Morn tug**
Tuesday	*Dienstag*	**Dean's tug**
Wednesday	*Mittwoch*	**Mitt voCH**
Thursday	*Donnerstag*	**Donna's tug**
Friday	*Freitag*	**Fry tug**
Saturday	*Samstag*	**Zam's tug**
Sunday	*Sonntag*	**Zon tug**
A day	*ein Tag*	**ine / Tug**
Two days	*zwei Tage*	**tss veye / Tugger**
A week	*eine Woche*	**eye ner / VOCH er**
A fortnight	*zwei Wochen*	**tss veye / VOCH en**
Three weeks	*drei Wochen*	**dry / VOCH en**

Months   *Monate*   Morn art er

A month	*ein Monat*	**ine / Morn art**
Two months	*zwei Monate*	**tss veye / Morn art er**
A year	*ein Jahr*	**ine / Yar**
Two years	*zwei Jahre*	**tss veye / Yah rer**
January	*Januar*	**Yan ooh ah**
February	*Februar*	**Feb roo ah**
March	*März*	**Mairts**
April	*April*	**Upril**
May	*Mai*	**My**
June	*Juni*	**You knee**
July	*Juli*	**You lee**
August	*August*	**Ow! goosed**
September	*September*	**Zept ember**
October	*Oktober*	**October**
November	*November*	**Naw vember**
December	*Dezember*	**Debts sember**

Spring	*Frühling*	**Froo ling**
Summer	*Sommer*	**Zommer**
Autum	*Herbst*	**Hair bst**
Winter	*Winter*	**Vinter**

Time   *Zeit*   Tsight

Midnight	*Mitternacht*	**Mitter naCHt**
Midday	*Mittag*	**Mitt tug**
Morning	*Morgen*	**More gun**
Afternoon	*Nachmittag*	**NaCH mitt tug**
Evening	*Abend*	**Are bent**

Nine o'clock *neun Uhr* **noin / Ooh err**

Quarter past nine *viertel nach neun* **fear till / naCH / noin**

Half past nine *halb neun* **hulp / noin**

Twenty to ten *zwanzig vor zehn* **tss vunt sig / for / tss zane**

Ten a.m. *zehn Uhr* **tss zane / Ooh err**

Ten p.m. *zweiundzwanzig Uhr* **tss veye oon tss vunt sig / Ooh err**

So now that you are joyfully familiar with using English to speak German you ought to be able to say:

On a winter's evening my mother-in-law cooked sauerkraut as she always does on a Tuesday. It had to be eaten at precisely seven o'clock, but as I was ten minutes late I had it served cold on the Wednesday.

An einem Winterabend kochte meine Schwiegermutter Sauerkraut wie jeden Dienstag. Es musste genau um sieben Uhr gegessen werden, aber da ich zehn Minuten zu spät kam, musste ich es am Mittwoch kalt essen.

Work out the pronunciation for yourself.

Emergencies   *Notfälle*   **Naught Feller**

Help!   *Hilfe!*   **Hill fir!**

Call for a doctor.
Rufen Sie einen Arzt.
Roof en / Zee / eye nen / Art st.

Call for an ambulance.
Rufen Sie einen Krankenwagen.
Roof en / Zee / eye nen / Crank en var gun.

Call for the police.
Rufen Sie die Polizei.
Roof en / Zee / dee / Pol its eye.

Call for a funeral director.
Rufen Sie einen Bestattungsunternehmer.
Roof en / Zee / eye nen / Be shh tat oong soon ter namer.

I am about to give birth; be sick; collapse.
Ich bin im Begriff, ein Kind zu bekommen; mich zu übergeben; zusammenzubrechen.
ICH / bin / im / Bug riff, / ine / Kint / ts zoo / beck common; miCH / ts zoo / oober gay ben; ts zoo salmon ts zoo breCHen.

I am allergic to prawns.
Ich bin allergisch gegen Krabben.
ICH / bin / al lair gish / gay gun / Crab ben.

Please contact my relatives. Their address is in my pocket.
Bitte benachrichtigen Sie meine Verwandten. Ihre Adresse ist in meiner Tasche.
Bitter / benaCH riCH tea gun / Zee / miner / Fair van ten / Ear rer / Address sir / ist / in / miner / Tasher.

I am with my best friend's wife. Please don't tell anybody.
Ich bin mit der Frau meines besten Freundes zusammen. Bitte sagen Sie es niemandem.
Ich / bin / mitt / dare / Frow! / minus / best ten / Froin dus / ts zoos ah men. / Bitter / zar gun / Zee / ess / knee mun dame.

At the Chemist
In der Apotheke **In dare / Ah pot tecker**

Chemists in Germany are medically knowledgeable and sometimes quite helpful if not over sympathetic to your ills. For minor problems consult them first.

Could I have a packet of – tissues – plasters – condoms?
Könnte ich eine – Packung Taschentücher – Pflaster; Präservative – haben?
Kern ter / iCH / eye ner – Puck oong / Tashen too CHer – Flaster – Pray serve vat tea fur – har ben?

14

What would you recommend for: ...?
Was empfehlen Sie gegen: ...
Vas / emp fail len / Zee / gay gun: ...

Migraine *Migräne* **Mee grainer**

Indigestion *Magenverstimmung* **Ma gun fair shh tim moong**

Menstruation pains *Menstruationsschmerzen* **Mens true at tea on shh mairt zen**

Insomnia *Schlaflosigkeit* **Shh laugh low zee kite**

Flatulence *Blähungen* **Blay oong gun**

Piles *Hämorrhoiden* **Hem or reed den**

High blood pressure *hohen Blutdruck* **hoe when / Bloot drook**

Irritable Bowel Syndrome
das gereizte-Eingeweide-Syndrom
duss / ger rights ter-Ine gerv eye der-Zindrom

I have a headache.
Ich habe Kopfschmerzen.
ICH / harbour / Kopf shh mairt zen.

I have a temperature.
Ich habe Fieber.
ICH / harbour / Fee ber.

I feel dizzy.
Mir ist schwindelig.
Mere / ist / shh vindle lick.

I have a sore throat.
Ich habe Halsschmerzen.
ICH / harbour / Halse shh mairt zen.

I have an awful cough.
Ich habe furchtbaren Husten.
ICH / harbour / forCHed bar wren / Houston.

I have bad blisters.
Ich habe schlimme Blasen.
ICH / harbour / shh limmer / Blaze en.

I've got dreadful diarrhoea.
Ich habe schrecklichen Durchfall.
ICH / harbour / shh wreck lickin' / DoorCH fall.

I am unspeakably constipated.
Ich habe unbeschreibliche Verstopfung.
ICH / harbour / oon besh rybe licker / Fair shh top foong.

At the Doctor *Beim Arzt* Bime / Art st

I have a serious – constant – spasmodic – pain in my …
Ich habe schlimme – beständige – sporadische – Schmerzen im … Bereich:
ICH / harbour / shh limmer / besh ten digger – shh poor ah disher – Shh mairt zen / im … / Bay rye CH:

Head	*Kopf*	**Kopf**
Ear	*Ohr*	**Oar**
Eye	*Auge*	**Ow! ger**
Neck	*Hals*	**Halss**
Shoulder	*Schulter*	**Shh oolter**
Heart	*Herz*	**Hairts**
Chest	*Brust*	**Broost**
Lungs	*Lungen*	**Loon gun**
Back	*Rücken*	**Rook ken**
Spine	*Rückgrat*	**Rook grat**

Stomach	*Magen*	**Mah gun**
Appendix	*Blinddarm*	**Blint darm**
Pancreas	*Bauchspeicheldrüse*	**Bow!CH spy shell drew sir**
Thigh	*Oberschenkel*	**Oh burr shenkel**
Leg	*Bein*	**Bine**
Knee	*Knie*	**Kenny**
Foot	*Fuss*	**Foos**
Toe	*Zeh*	**Tseh**
Rectum	*Mastdarm*	**Must darm**
Genitals	*Genitalien*	**Gay knee tar lee en**

NB. If the painful area is not listed – point.

I am accused of being a hypochondriac but I am sure I am suffering from Munchhausen syndrome.
Man wirft mir vor, ein Hypochonder zu sein, aber ich bin sicher, dass ich an dem Münchhausen-Syndrom leide.
Mun / veer ft / mere / for / ine / Hippo honder / ts zoo / zine / arbour / iCH / bin / ziCHer / duss / iCH / un / dame / Moon shh how! zen / Zin drom / lie der.

I have had stomach pains for the last week.
Ich habe seit einer Woche Magenschmerzen.
ICH / harbour / zite / eye ner / VoCH er / Mar gun shh mairt zen.

I have been spitting blood.
Ich habe Blut gespuckt.
ICH / harbour/ Bloot / gesh pookt.

My poo-poo is black – brown – beige – green.
Mein Stuhl ist schwarz – braun – beige – grün.
Mine / Shh tool / ist / shh varts – brown – beige – groon.

I think I am going to die.
Ich glaube, ich sterbe.
ICH / glow! ber, / iCH / shh terber.

Are you sure that my symptoms are caused by stress?
Sind Sie sicher, dass meine Symptome vom Stress herrühren?
Zint / Zee / ziCHer / duss / miner / Zimp toe mer / fom / Stress / hair roo wren?

At the Hospital
Im Krankenhaus **Im / Crank en house**

I think there are fleas inside my plaster.
Ich glaube, da sind Flöhe unter meinem Gips.
ICH / glow! ber, / dah / zint / Flewer / oon ter / my nem / Gips.

I am suffering terribly. Could I have morphine?
Ich leide schrecklich. Könnte ich Morphium bekommen?
ICH / lie der / shh wreck lick. / Kern ter / iCH / Morphium / beck common?

That was nice. Could I have another shot?
Das war gut. Könnte ich noch eine Spritze bekommen?
Duss / var / goot / kern ter / iCH / noCH / eye ner / Shh prit sir / beck common?

I do not want another blanket bath.
Ich will nicht schon wieder gewaschen werden.
ICH / vill / niCHt / shone / veeder / gay vashen / vair den.

I need a bedpan urgently.
Ich brauche dringend eine Bettpfanne.
ICH / brow! CHer / dring ghent / eye ner / Bet puf anna.

Could you give me another pillow?
Könnten Sie mir noch ein Kissen geben?
Kern ten / Zee / mere / noch / ine / Kissen / gay ben.

18

My mother-in-law is coming to visit me. Could you tell her I am in a coma?
Meine Schwiegermutter kommt mich besuchen. Könnten Sie ihr bitte sagen, dass ich im Koma liege?
Miner / Shh veeg air mooter / komt / miCH / buzz zoo CHen. / Kern ten / Zee / ear / bitter / zar gun / duss / iCH / im / Coma / league er?

When can I leave?
Wann kann ich nach Hause?
Van / cun / iCH / naCH / How! sir?

At the Optician *Beim Optiker* Bime / Op ticker

I have broken my spectacles. Can you replace them?
Ich habe meine Brille zerbrochen. Können Sie sie ersetzen?
ICH / harbour / miner / Briller / tsir broCH en. / Ker nun / Zee / zee / air zet zen?

I have lost one of my contact lenses.
Ich habe eine meiner Kontaktlinsen verloren.
ICH / harbour / eye ner / miner / Contact lin zen / fair law wren.

It fell into the sauerkraut and disappeared.
Sie ist ins Sauerkraut gefallen und verschwunden.
Zee / ist / ince / Sour krow!t / gef fallen / oont / fair shh voon den.

I am myopic – long sighted.
Ich bin kurzsichtig – weitsichtig.
ICH / bin / courts ziCH tig – vite ziCH tig.

What chart where?
Welche Tabelle und wo?
Velch er / Tabella / oont / vo?

At the Dentist *Beim Zahnarzt* Bime / Tss arn art st

I have cronic toothache.
Ich habe chronische Zahnschmerzen.
Ich / harbour / crow knee sher / Ts arn shh mairt sen.

I have lost a filling.
Ich habe eine Plombe verloren.
Ich / harbour / eye ner / Plum burr / fair law wren.

My gums are sore.
Mein Zahnfleisch ist wund.
Mine / Ts arn fly shh / ist / voont.

That hurts!
Das tut weh!
Duss / toot / veh!

Of course I want an anaesthetic.
Natürlich will ich eine Narkose.
Nat ewer lich / vill / ich / eye ner / Narcosa.

Where do I spit?
Wo soll ich es ausspucken?
Vo / zoll / ich / ess / ow! shh poo ken?

Should my tooth have come out like that?
Sollte mein Zahn so rausgekommen sein?
Zalter / mine / Tss arn / zo / row!ss geck common / sign?

Getting About

On Foot   *Zu Fuss*   **Ts zoo / Fooss**

Which way is North – South – East – West?
Wo ist Norden – Süden – Osten – Westen?
Vo / ist / Nor den – Zoo den – Os ten – Vest ten?

Where is …?   *Wo ist … ?*   **Vo ist … ?**

You should be prepared to receive such answers as:

Vo hin / gay en / Zee?
Wohin gehen Sie?
Where are you going?

Ess / ist / vite / fon / here.
Es ist weit von hier.
It's a long way from here.

Vo ist …?

21

Ess / ist / niCHt / vite.
Es ist nicht weit.
It isn't far.

Gay en / Zee / immer / ger ardour ow!ss.
Gehen Sie immer geradeaus.
Keep straight on.

Gay en / Zee / links.
Gehen Sie links.
Turn left.

Gay en / Zee / reCH ts.
Gehen Sie rechts.
Turn right.

Gay en / Zee / dane / Vague / ts zoo rook, / dane / Zee / geck common / zint.
Gehen Sie den Weg zurück, den Sie gekommen sind.
Go back the way you came.

If you do not understand this because of rural accents try:

Can you show me where that is on the map?
Können Sie mir auf der Karte zeigen, wo das liegt?
Ker nun / Zee / mere / ow!f / dare / Carter / ts eye gun / vo / duss / leaked?

Can you draw it for me please?
Können Sie mir das bitte aufzeichnen?
Ker nun / Zee / mere / duss / bitter / ow!f ts eyeCH nen?

Where is the nearest taxi rank?
Wo ist der nächste Taxistand?
Vo / ist / dare / neCH ster / Taxi shh tunt?

By Taxi   *Mit dem Taxi*   Mitt / dame / Taxi

The main station, please.
Zum Hauptbahnhof bitte.
Ts zoom / How!pt barn hoff / bitter.

Unless your destination is well known, it is best to write down the address you want to go to. After which you should keep quiet and listen enraptured to Dietrich Fischer-Dieskau belting out Götterdammerung on the driver's superlative quadrophonic sound system.

By Train   *Mit dem Zug*   Mitt /dame / Ts zoog

Station *Bahnhof* **Barn hoff**
Main station *Hauptbahnhof* **How!pt barn hoff**
Platform *Bahnsteig* **Barn shh tie g**

Nahverkehrszug – Painfully slow, stopping at every station
Regionalzug – Stops at most stations
Expresszug – Rapid train, waits for no-one

What time are the train departures for Stuttgart?
Um wieviel Uhr fahren die Züge nach Stuttgart ab?
Um / vee feel / oor / far ren / dee / Ts zoo ger / naCH / Stoot gart / up?

One ticket for Bielefeld.
Eine Fahrkarte nach Bielefeld.
Eye ner / Far carter / naCH / Beeler felt.

Two return tickets to Würzburg.
Zwei Rückfahrkarten nach Würzburg.
Tss veye / Rook far carton / naCH / Verts boorg.

Do I have to change?
Muss ich umsteigen?
Moose / iCH / oom shh tie gun?

Which platform for Berlin?
Auf welchem Gleis fährt der Zug nach Berlin ab?
Ow!f / velCH em / glice / fairt / dare / Ts zoog / naCH / Bare lean / up?

What station is this?
Was für eine Station ist das?
Vass / fewer / eye ner / shh tat see on / ist / duss?

I wanted to get out at Garmisch-Partenkirchen.
Ich wollte in Garmisch-Partenkirchen aussteigen.
Ich / volt er / in / Garmish-Parten keer CHen / ow!ss shh tie gun.

Where does this train go to then?
Wohin fährt denn dieser Zug?
Vo hin / fairt / den / dee sir / Ts zoog?

I know it's not the right ticket!
Ich weiß, dass das nicht die richtige Fahrkarte ist!
ICH / vice, / duss / duss / niCHt / dee / riCH tigger / Far carter / ist!

How much more?
Wie hoch ist der Aufpreis?
Vee / hoCH / ist / dare / Ow!f price?

Do you accept roubles?
Nehmen Sie auch Rubel?
Nemun / Zee / ow!CH / Rooble?

By Bus *Mit dem Bus* Mitt / dame / Boos

Where can I get a bus for Baden-Baden?
Wo fährt der Bus nach Baden-Baden ab?
Vo / fairt / dare / Boos / naᴄʜ / Bar den Bar den / up?

Does this bus stop at the market?
Hält dieser Bus am Markt?
Helt / dee sir / Boos / am / Mark tt?

Could you tell me where I get off?
Könnten Sie mir sagen, wo ich aussteigen muss?
Kern ten / Zee / mere / zar gun / vo / iᴄʜ / ow!ss shh tie gun / moose?

How long does it take to get to Bad Kissingen?
Wie lange dauert die Fahrt nach Bad Kissingen?
Vee / lung er / dow! ert / dee / fart / naᴄʜ / Bart Kissing gun?

I was told this bus went to Bad Kreuznach.
Man hat mir gesagt, dieser Bus fährt nach Bad Kreuznach.
Mun / hut / mere / gez act / dee sir / Boos / fairt / naᴄʜt / Bart Kroits naᴄʜ.

I am on the wrong bus. Please stop, I want to get off.
Ich bin im falschen Bus. Könnten Sie bitte anhalten, ich möchte aussteigen.
Iᴄʜ / bin / im / false shun / Boos. / Kern ten / Zee / bitter / an halten / iᴄʜ / murᴄʜter / ow!ss shh tie gun.

When is the next bus back to Munich?
Wann fährt der nächste Bus zurück nach München?
Van / fairt / dare / naᴄʜ stir / Boos / ts zoo rook / naᴄʜ / Moon shen?

Is there any other way I can get to Munich?
Gibt es irgendeine andere Möglichkeit nach München zu kommen?
Geept / ess / ear ghent eye ner / under er / Murg liᴄʜ kite / naᴄʜ / Moon shen / ts zoo / common?

By River Boat *Durch Dampfer* Durᴄʜ / Dam fir

Is this gangplank safe?
Is diese Laufplanke sicher?
Ist / dee sir / Low!f planker / ziᴄʜ er?

I feel sick.
Mir ist schlecht.
Mere / ist / shh leᴄʜt.

Should we be at this angle?
Müssen wir in diesem Winkel liegen?
Moosen / vere / in / dee sem / Vinkle / lee gun?

I can't swim.
Ich kann nicht schwimmen.
Iᴄʜ / can / niᴄʜt / shh vim men.

Have you got a life jacket?
Haben Sie eine Schwimmweste?
Har ben / Zee / eye ner / shh vim vester?

Man overboard! *Mann über Bord!* **Mun / oober / board!**

Are you sure I need a tetanus injection?
Muss ich unbedingt gegen Tetanus geimpft werden?
Muss / iᴄʜ / oon bed inked / gay gun / Tetanoos / gay impft / vair den?

26

By Car   *Mit dem Auto*   Mitt / dame / Ow! toe

Car rental agency
Autovermietung   **Ow!toe fair meet toong**

I want to rent a car.
Ich möchte ein Auto mieten.
Ich / murch ter / ine / Ow! toe / meet ten.

Do you have any other colours? I find khaki a bit dull.
Haben Sie noch andere Farben? Khaki finde ich ein wenig langweilig.
Har ben / Zee / noch / under er / Farben? / Khaki / fin der / ich / ine / vain nig / lung vile lig.

What type of petrol does the car consume?
Was für Benzin braucht das Auto?
Vass / fewer / Bent seen / brow! cht / duss / Ow! toe?

Petrol station   *Tankstelle*   **Tank shh teller**

Unleaded   *Bleifrei*   **Bly fry**
Super   *Super*   **Zooper**
Diesel   *Diesel*   **Diesel**

Could you give me a full tank please.
Einmal volltanken, bitte.
Ine mal / foll tanken / bitter.

I would like ten litres.
Ich hätte gerne zehn Liter.
Ich / hetter / gair ner / tss sane / Leeter.

Ten Euro worth of petrol please.
Für zehn Euro Benzin bitte.
Fewer / tss sane / Oi roe / Bent seen / bitter.

Car Trouble   *Auto Probleme*   **Ow! toe / Prob lemmer**

I have locked the keys inside the car.
Ich habe die Schlüssel im Auto eingeschlossen.
Iᴄʜ / harbour / dee / shh loo sell / im / Ow! toe / ine ger shloss en.

I have run out of petrol.
Ich habe kein Benzin mehr.
Iᴄʜ / harbour / kine / Bent seen / mare.

Where is the nearest garage for repairs?
Wo ist die nächste Werkstatt?
Vo / ist / dee / naᴄʜ stir / Vark shh tart?

I have a puncture.
Ich habe einen Platten.
Iᴄʜ / harbour / eye nen / Platten.

I have engine trouble.
Ich habe Motorprobleme.
Iᴄʜ / harbour / Motor problem er.

How long will it take?
Wie lange wird es dauern?
Vee / lung ger / veert / ess / dow! urn?

When can I collect it?
Wann kann ich es abholen?
Vun / cun / iᴄʜ / ess / up holen?

Are you sure this is correct? My car is not a Ferrari!
Sind Sie sicher, dass das richtig ist? Mein Auto ist kein Ferrari!
Zint / Zee / ziᴄʜer, / duss / duss / riᴄʜ tig / ist? / Mine / Ow! toe / ist / kine / Ferrari!

Where can I hire a Volkswagen beetle?
Wo kann ich einen Volkswagen Käfer mieten?
Vo / cun / iCH / eye nen / Folks vah gun / Kef fir / meet ten?

Road Rage   *Straßen-Raserei*   Strah sen / Rass sir eye

Road rage is not tolerated by the police in Germany, so check that there are no law officers around before losing your cool.

What are you hooting at?
Warum zur Hölle hupen Sie?
Varoom / ts zur / Her ler / hoopen / Zee?

Why don't you learn to drive!
Lern erstmal fahren, du!
Lairn / airst mal / far run, / doo!

The left indicator meant that I was going to turn left, you plonker!
Der linke Blinker bedeutet, dass ich links abbiegen will, du Flasche!
Dare / link er / Blink er / bay doit tet / duss / iCH / links / up bee gun / vill, / doo / Flusher!

I didn't know it was a one way street!
Ich wusste nicht, dass dies eine Einbahnstraße ist!
ICH / vooster / niCHt, / duss / dees / eye ner / Ine barn strasser / ist!

Here are some choice words that may be shouted at you by angry German drivers:

Blurred mun! *Blödmann!* Idiot!

Shh vye ner hoont! *Schweinehund!* Bastard! (Literally, pig dog)

Shy sir! *Scheiße!* Shit!

Dreck eager / ulter / shh voo lee!
Dreckiger alter Schwuli!
Dirty old poofter!

Ow!ss / dame / Vague, / Arse shh loCH!
Aus dem Weg, Arschloch!
Get out of the way, arsehole!

To which you may care to reply:

And the same to you! (Literally: You are one!)
Selber einer!
Zel ber / eye ner!

Parking   *Parkplatz*   Park plats

The ticket machine does not work.
Die Parkuhr funktioniert nicht.
Dee / Parker / foonk tsee on knee urt / niCHt.

I do not understand the instructions.
Ich verstehe die Anweisungen nicht.
ICH / fair shh tayer / dee / Un vice oong gun / niCHt.

Which slot?
Welcher Schlitz?
Vel CHer / Shh lits?

The barrier will not go up.
Die Schranke geht nicht hoch.
Dee / Shrunk er / gate / niCHt / hoCH.

I cannot find my car.
Ich kann meinen Wagen nicht finden.
ICH / cun / mine nen / Vah gun / niCHt / fin den.

I do not remember the number.
Ich erinnere mich nicht an die Nummer.
ICH / air inner ruh / miCH / niCHt / an / dee / Noomer.

I will know it when I see it.
Wenn ich ihn sehe, erkenne ich ihn.
Ven / iCH / een / zayer, / air kenner / iCH / een.

In the car next to mine, a Rottweiler was ripping up the back seat.
Im Auto neben meinem hat ein Rottweiler den Rücksitz kaputtgemacht.
Im / Ow! toe / nay ban / mine em / hut / ine / Rot vile ler / dane / Rook zits / kaputt gay muCHt.

Shy sir!

Getting a Room

Five Star
There should be no need to speak German in a five star hotel. Receptionists, head waiters, waiters, barmen, bell-boys and chambermaids have to speak English.

Four Star
There should be no need to speak German in a four star hotel. Receptionists, head waiters, and barmen are ordered to speak English.

Three Star
There should be no need to speak German in a three star hotel. The receptionist and the head waiter have to speak English, and other members of the staff will be learning it, intent on promotion.

Two Star
The receptionist may be under the impression that he or she speaks English, but in fact is quite unintelligible. Best to arm yourself with a phrase book to get what you really want.

One Star
These hotels cater mainly for the natives. The owner manager will deliberately not understand you if his BMW was overtaken by a British car on the autobahn that morning.

Certain phrases may be useful in all or any hotels:

Do you have a single room?
Haben Sie ein Einzelzimmer frei?
Har ben / Zee / ine / Ine cell ts simmer / fry?

I would like a double room for three nights.
Ich hätte gerne ein Doppelzimmer für drei Nächte.
Ich / hetter / gair ner / ine / Dopple ts simmer / fewer / dry / Nech ter.

At what time do you start – stop – serving breakfast?
Von wann bis – wann gibt – es Frühstück?
Fon / vun / biss – vun / geept – ess / Froo shh took?

Are there any messages for me?
Sind irgendwelche Nachrichten für mich da?
Zint / ear gunt velCH er / NaCH riCH ten / fewer / miCH / da?

I am leaving tomorrow.
Ich fahre morgen ab.
ICH / far rer / more gun / up.

What is the weather forecast?
Wie ist die Wettervorhersage?
Vee / ist / dee / Vetter for hair sayger?

What are these charges for?
Wofür sind diese Gebühren?
Vo fewer / zint / dee sir / Gay boo wren?

But there are no phones in your rooms, and I have a mobile anyway.
Aber es gibt keine Telefone auf den Zimmern, und ich habe sowieso ein Handy.
Arbour / ess / geept / kye ner / Telephoner / ow!f / dane / Tsim urn, / oont / iCH / harbour / zo vee zo / ine / Handy.

No Star
The owner manager will not understand a word you say whether you use this book or not, but try:

I would like to have a bath. Can I have the bathplug
please?
*Ich würde gerne ein Bad nehmen. Könnte ich bitte den
Badewannenstöpsel haben?*
**ICH / verder / gairner / ine / Bat / naymen. / Kern ter /
iCH / bitter / dane / Bar day van en stirp sell / har ben?**

Is the water traditionally brown in this area?
Ist das Wasser üblicherweise braun in dieser Gegend?
**Ist / duss / Vasser / oop lee cHer visor / brown / in / dee
sir / Gay ghent?**

Does your son always only dedicate himself to the flugel-
horn at night?
Tut ihr Sohn nachts nichts anderes als Flügelhorn spielen?
**Toot / ear / Zon / naCHts / niCHts / under ess / als /
Floogel horn / shh pee len?**

Getting Service

At the Bookshop; Stationer; Newsagent

Buchladen **Booch larden**;
Schreibwarenhandlung **Shh rybe vah wren hunt loong**;
Zeitungshändler **Tsight oongs hentler**

Do you have any local guide books?
Haben Sie einen Reiseführer für diese Gegend?
**Har ben / Zee / eye nen / Riser few rer / fewer / dee sir /
Gay ghent?**

Have you any maps of the city?
Haben Sie Stadtpläne?
Har ben / Zee / Shh tat plainer?

34

Do you have this in English?
Haben Sie dieses auf Englisch?
Har ben / Zee / dee zizz / ow!f / En glish?

Do you have any English newspapers?
Haben Sie englische Zeitungen?
Har ben / Zee / en glisher / Tsight oon gun?

Do you have any nudie magazines?
Haben Sie Nacktmagazine?
Har ben / Zee / Naсht maggot seen er?

I wasn't trying to pinch it, I just didn't want my wife to know I was buying it.
Ich habe nicht versucht, es zu klauen, ich wollte nur nicht, dass meine Frau weiß, dass ich es kaufe.
Iсh / harbour / niсht / fair zooсht, / ess / ts zoo / klow! en / iсh / vol ter / noor / niсht, / duss / miner / Frow! vice / duss / iсh / ess / cow! fur.

At the Post Office *Auf der Post* Ow!f / dare / Poss tt

Post offices in Germany are extremely efficient, and in the larger ones a foreign language speaking official has usually been appointed to see to your dire needs should you have them.

How much is a stamp for this?
Wieviel kostet eine Briefmarke hierfür?
Vee feel / cost et / eye ner / Brief marker / here fewer?

Will these postcards go today?
Werden die Postkarten noch heute verschickt?
Vair den / die / Posst cart ten / noсh / hoiter / fair shick tt?

When will they get there?
Wann werden sie ankommen?
Van / vair den / zee / un common?

I wish to register this parcel.
Ich möchte dieses Paket per Einschreiben schicken.
Iᴄʜ / murᴄʜter / dee zizz / Peck ate / pair / Ine shh rye ben / she ken.

That is expensive. I don't have any more money.
Das ist teuer. Ich habe nicht mehr Geld.
Duss / ist / toy er. / Iᴄʜ / harbour / niᴄʜt / mare / Gelt.

Which window do I go to then?
Zu welchem Schalte muss ich denn gehen?
Ts zoo / velᴄʜ em / Shelter / moose / iᴄʜ / den / gay en?

I have just been there and they told me to come here!
Da war ich gerade und man hat mir gesagt, ich solle hier herkommen!
Da / var / iᴄʜ / ger ardour / oont / mun / hat / mere / gay zaᴄʜt, / iᴄʜ / zoller / here / hair common!

This parcel is fragile. Please be careful.
Der Inhalt dieses Päckchens ist zerbrechlich. Bitte seien Sie vorsichtig.
Der / In halt / dee zizz / Peck ᴄʜens / ist / tser breᴄʜ liᴄʜ. / Bitter / sigh en / Zee / for ziᴄʜ tig.

Good Grief! *Du liebe Güte!*
Doo / lee ber / Gooter!

It wasn't rattling before you franked it.
Es hat nicht geklappert, bevor Sie es gestempelt haben.
Es / hat / niᴄʜt / geck lap pert, / before / Zee / ess / guess temp pelt / har ben.

Could I have it back please?
Könnte ich es bitte zurückhaben?
Kern ter / icH / ess / bitter / ts zoo rook har ben?

At the Bank   *Auf der Bank*   **Auf / dare / Bunk**

I wish to change these travellers cheques.
Ich möchte bitte diese Reiseschecks einlösen.
**IcH / murcH ter / bitter / dee sir / Riser shex / ine ler
zen.**

What is the rate of exchange?
Wie ist der Wechselkurs?
Vee / ist / dare / VecH sel course?

The cash point has swallowed my card.
Der Geldautomat hat meine Karte geschluckt.
**Der / Gelt ow! toe mart / hat / miner / Carter / guess shh
looked.**

I cashed money with it yesterday.
Ich habe erst gestern Geld damit abgehoben.
**IcH / harbour / airst / guess tairn / Gelt / dammit / up
gay hoe ben.**

No, I have not spent my limit for today.
*Nein, ich habe nicht mein Limit für heute bereits über-
schritten.*
**Nine / icH / harbour / nicHt / mine / Limit / fewer /
hoiter / buh rights / oober shh written.**

I would like to talk to the manager.
Könnte ich bitte den Geschäftsleiter sprechen?
**Kern ter / icH / bitter / dane / Gay shefts lighter /
shh precH en.**

Could I ring my bank at home?
Könnte ich meine Bank anrufen?
Kern ter / iᴄʜ / miner / Bunk / un roofen?

Where do I sign?
Wo muss ich unterschreiben?
Vo / moose / iᴄʜ / oonter shh rye ben?

At the Hairdresser *Beim Frisör* Bime / Freeze ewer

Vee / het ten / Zee / ess / gair ner?
Wie hätten Sie es gerne?
How would you like it?

Wash and blow dry.
Waschen und fönen.
Va shun / oont / fur nen.

But I didn't want it cut at all!
Aber ich wollte es überhaupt nicht geschnitten haben!
Arbour / iᴄʜ / vol ter / ess / oober how!pt / niᴄʜt / guess shh knit ten / har ben!

At the Barber
Beim Herrenfriseur Bime / Heron freeze ewer

You want it short?
Möchten Sie es kurz?
Murᴄʜ ten / Zee / ess / courts?

Quite short. *Ziemlich kurz.* **Tseem liᴄʜ / courts.**
Not too short. *Nicht zu kurz.* **Niᴄʜt / ts zoo / courts.**

A little bit off the sides.
An den Seiten ein wenig ab.
An / dane / Sigh ten / ine / vain nig / up.

Were you trained as a hairdresser in the army?
Sind Sie bei der Armee zum Friseur ausgebildet worden?
Zint / Zee / by / dare / Armay / ts zoom / Freeze ewer / ow!ss ger built et / vor den?

Getting Something to Eat and Drink

At the Café   *Am Café*   **Am / Café**

I would like a black coffee please.
Ich möchte einen schwarzen Kaffee bitte.
ICH / murCH ter / eye nen / shh vart sen / Café / bitter.

Coffee with milk   *Kaffee mit Milch*   **Café / mitt / Mill CH**
Tea with milk   *Tee mit Milch*   **Tay / mitt / Mill CH**

Decafinated coffee
Koffeinfreier Kaffee   **Kof fine fryer / Café**

A cup of hot chocolate please.
Eine Tasse heiße Schokolade bitte.
Eye ner / Tass sir / high sir / Shock oh larder / bitter.

Could I have more sugar?
Können Sie mir mehr Zucker geben?
Ker nun / Zee / mere / mare / Ts zoo cur / gay ben?

What cakes do you have?
Was für Kuchen haben Sie?
Vas / fewer / Koo CHen / har ben / Zee?

I would like a slice of marzipan cake.
Ich hätte gerne ein Stück Marzipankuchen.
ICH / hetter / gair ner / ine / Shh took / Mart see pan koo CHen.

Now I would like to try your Black Forest cake.
Jetzt möchte ich gern Ihre Schwarzwälder Kirschtorte kosten.
Yet st / merCH te / iCH / gairn / Ear rer / Shh varts veil dare / Kirsh torter / cost en.

And to finish, I will have Applestrudel and a slice of Sachetorte.
Und zum Abschluss hätte ich gern Apfelstrudel, und ein Stück Sachertorte.
Oont / ts zoom / Up shh loose / hetter / iCH / gairn / Ap fell stroo dell, / oont / ine / Shh took / ZaCHer torter.

Could you bring me a doggy bag?
Könnten Sie mir bitte eine Plastiktüte fur meinen Hund geben?
Kern ten / Zee / mere / bitter / eye ner / Plastic tooter / for / mine nen / Hoont / gay ben?

Fast Food *Schnellimbiss* **Shh nell imbiss**

Hamburger	*Hamburger*	**Ham boor ger**
Sausage	*Wurst*	**Vorst**

Ice Cream	*Eiscreme*	**Ice crem**
Milk Shake	*Milchshake*	**MilCH shake**

Flavour: Strawberry; Chocolate
Geschmack: Erdbear; Schokolade
Guess shh muck: **Eart bare; Shock oh larder**

I would like a sandwich (literally 'laid down bread'):
ham; cheese; salami; pork; beef; chicken; tuna fish.
Ich möchte ein belegtes Brot: Schinken; Käse; Salami;
Schweinefleisch; Rind; Hühnchen; Thunfisch.
ICH / murCH ter / ine / bell egg tess / Brought: Shinken;
Kay zer; Salami; Shh vye ner fly shh; Rint; Hoon shen;
Toon fish.

Slow Food

Breakfast	*Frühstück*	**Froo shh took**
Lunch	*Mittagessen*	**Mitt tug essen**
Dinner	*Abendessen*	**Are bent essen**
Supper	*Nachtimbiss*	**NaCH tim biss**

Starters	*Vorspeisen*	**For spy zen**
Soup	*Suppe*	**Zoo per**
Fish	*Fisch*	**Fish**
Meat	*Fleisch*	**Fly shh**
Vegetable	*Gemüse*	**Gay mooser**
Cheese	*Käse*	**Kay zer**
Dessert	*Nachtisch*	**NaCH tish**

I'll have the Thüringen sausages and mashed potato, and
my friend will have the venison.
Ich nehme Thüringer Rostbratwurst mit Kartoffelbrei, und
mein Freund nimmt den Rehbraten.
ICH / name er / dee / Tour ringer / Rost brart vorst / mitt /
Cart offal bry, / oont / mine / Froind / nimt / dane /
Ray bra ten.

I have changed my mind.
Ich habe mich anders entschlossen.
ICH / harbour / miCH / unders / ent shh loss en.

41

I'll have what he's having.
Ich hätte gern dasselbe wie der Herr da.
ICH / hetter / gairn / duss sell ber / vee / dare / Hair / da.

Duss / ist / alice / fewer / hoiter.
Das ist alles für heute.
That is finished for the day.

Then I'll have the pork knuckle with pickled cabbage and mushy peas.
Dann möchte ich gerne Eisbein mit Sauerkraut und Erbsbrei.
Done / murCH ter / iCH / gair ner / Ice bine / mitt / Sour kraut / oont / Airbs bry.

We would like another plate to share a portion.
Wir hätten gern noch einen Teller um uns das Essen zu teilen.
Were / het ten / gairn / noCH / eye nen / teller / oom / oons duss / Essen / ts zoo / tile en.

42

Essential Questions for Waiters

Waiter   *Herr Ober*   **Hair / Oh burr**
Waitress   *Fräulein*   **Froi line**

Could you recommend a good local wine?
Können Sie einen guten hiesigen Wein empfehlen?
Ker nun / Zee / eye nen / goo ten / he see gun / Vine / emp fay len?

A glass of white wine – red wine.
Ein Glas Weißwein – Rotwein.
Ine / Glass / Vice vine – Rot vine.

Mineral water   *Mineralwasser*   **Mineral vasser**
Sparkling   *Mit Kohlensäure*   **Mitt / Colon zoirer**
Still   *Ohne Kohlensäure*   **Owner / Colon zoirer**

I have been waiting a long time for my food.
Ich warte schon sehr lange auf mein Essen.
ICH / vart er / shone / zare / lung ger / ow!f / mine / Essen.

The bill please.
Die Rechnung, bitte.
Dee / reCH noong, / bitter.

This is not correct.
Das ist nicht korrekt.
Duss / ist / niCHt / correct.

Is the tip included?
Ist das Trinkgeld mit inbegriffen?
Ist / duss / Trink gelt / mitt / in bug griffen?

Have you got a toothpick?
Haben Sie einen Zahnstocher?
Har ben / Zee / eye nen / Tsar ens toCH er?

Having Fun

At the Opera   *Am Oper*   **Am / Oh per**

Box Office	*Kartenschalter*	**Carton shall tar**
Stalls	*Parkett*	**Park it**
Circle	*Rang*	**Rung**
Gods	*Gallerie*	**Gallery**

Two seats for tonight.
Zwei Plätze für heute Abend.
Tss veye / Plets zer / fewer / hoiter / are bent.

I have been queueing for two hours and now you tell me there are no seats?
Ich stehe schon zwei Stunden Schlange, und jetzt sagen Sie mir, dass keine Plätze mehr frei sind?
ICH / shh tayer / shone / tss veye / Shh toon den / Shh lung ger, / oont / yet st / zar gun / Zee / mere, / duss / kye ner / Plets zer / mare / fry / zint?

I would like a box for Saturday's performance.
Ich hätte gerne eine Loge für die Vorstellung am nächsten Samstag.
ICH / hetter / gairner / eye ner / Lowj er / fewer / dee / For shh tell oong / am / next ten / Zam's tug.

Give me a programme please.
Geben Sie mir ein Programm, bitte.
Gay ben / Zee / mere / ine / Programme / bitter.

I believe you are sitting in my seat.
Ich glaube, Sie sitzen auf meinem Platz.
ICH / glow!ber / Zee / zits zen / ow!f / mine em / Plats.

Shopping *Einkaufen* Ine cow! fin

What day is the street market?
Wann ist Markttag?
Van / ist / marked tug?

How much is the beer mug with the big lid?
Was kostet der Bierkrug mit dem großen Deckel?
Vass / costet / dare / Beer kroog / mitt / dame / gross urn / Deckle?

How much!?
Wieviel!?
Vee feel!?

Is that the best price you can give?
Ist das Ihr bester Preis?
Ist / duss / Ear / best er / Price?

I'll leave it.
Ich nehme es nicht.
ICH / name er / ess / niCHt.

Is this is a genuine piece of the Berlin Wall?
Ist das ein echtes Stück von der Berliner Mauer?
Ist / duss / ine / eCH tess / Shh took / von / dare / Bear leaner / Mow! er?

I'll take it.
Ich nehme es.
ICH / name er / es.

Can you tell me where I can hire a truck?
Können Sie mir sagen, wo ich einen Laster mieten kann?
Ker nun / Zee / mere / zar gun, / vo / iCH / eye nen / Lust ter / meet ten / cun?

At the Department Store

Im Kaufhaus   Im / Cow!f house

Where will I find the lift – the escalator?
Wo finde ich den Fahrstuhl – die Rolltreppe?
Vo / fin der / iCH / den / far shh tool – dee / roll trepper?

May I try this on?
Könnte ich es anprobieren?
Kern ter / iCH / ess / an pro beer en?

Where is the changing room?
Wo ist die Umkleidekabine?
Vo / ist / dee / Oom clyde er cab bean er?

I don't like the colour.
Die Farbe gefällt mir nicht.
Dee / Farber / gay felt / mere / niCHt.

It doesn't fit me.
Es passt mir nicht.
Ess / past / mere / niCHt.

It is too big – too small – too wide – too tight.
Es ist zu groß – zu klein – zu weit – zu eng.
Es / ist / tszoo / gross / – ts zoo / kline – ts zoo / veit – ts zoo / eng.

I cannot get it off.
Ich kriege es nicht ab.
ICH / cree ger / ess / niCHt / up.

Please calm down. I will pay for the damages.
Beruhigen Sie sich. Ich bezahle den Schaden.
Bay roo ee gun / Zee / ziCH. / ICH / bazaar ler / dane / Shah den.

Sight Seeing *Die Besichtigung* Dee / Buzz iCH tea gung

At what time does this art gallery open – shut?
Um wieviel Uhr öffnet – schließt – diese Kunstgallerie?
Oom / vee feel / Oo err / erf net – shh leased – dee sir / Coonst gallery?

Of any painting, loudly:

I think its pre-occupation with fundamentals is perverse.
Meiner Meinung nach ist seine Vorliebe für das Grundlegende pervers.
Miner / Mine ung / nach / ist / zye ner / For lee burr / fewer / duss / Grunt lay gun der / per fairs.

If the Cathedral is not open today, when does it open?
Wenn der Dom heute nicht öffnet, wann ist er überhaupt offen?
Ven / dare / Dome / hoiter / niCHt / erf net, / van / ist / air / oober how!pt / off fen?

Can I go round the castle alone or do I have to join the tour?
Kann ich mich im Schloss alleine umschauen, oder muss ich mich einer Führung anschließen?
Can / iCH / miCH / im / Shh loss / al liner / oomsh ow! en, / odour / moose / iCH / miCH / eye ner / Fewer wrong / an shh lee sen?

When does it start?
Um wieviel Uhr fängt es an?
Oom / vee feel / Ooh err / feng tt / ess / an?

Which way do I go?
Wie kommt man dahin?
Vee / kom tt / mun / da hin?

The tour has gone? But I am only a few seconds late!
Die Gruppe ist schon weg? Aber ich bin doch nur ein paar Sekunden zu spät!
Dee / Grooper / ist / shone / vague? / Arbour / iCH / bin / doch / noor / ine / par / Seck oon den / ts zoo / shh pate!

At the Spa *Im Kurhaus* Im / Coo er house

I would like a massage and sauna to follow.
Ich hätte gerne eine Massage mit anschließendem Saunagang.
ICH / hetter / gairner / eye ner / Massager / mitt / un shh lee send em / Zow!na gung.

How much is the session?
Wieviel kostet eine Sitzung?
Vee feel / cost et / eye ner / Zits zoong?

Can you do that again?
Können Sie das noch einmal machen?
Ker nun / Zee / duss / noch / ine mal / maCH en?

Not quite so hard this time.
Nicht ganz so doll dieses Mal.
NiCHt / gants / zo / doll / dee zizz / Mal.

The steam is far too hot for me.
Der Dampf ist mir viel zu heiß.
Dare / Dampf / ist / mere / feel / ts zoo / high ss.

I must get out of here!
Ich muss hier raus!
ICH / moose / here / row! ss!

Walking   *Spazieren*   Ssh pats ear ran

Excuse me, but do you know where we are?
Entschuldigung, aber wissen Sie, wo wir sind?
Ent shool dig goong, / arbour / vissen / Zee, / vo / vere / zint?

We have lost the group leader.
Wir haben den Gruppenleiter verloren.
Veer / har ben / dane / Groupen lighter / fair law wren.

I can't find my way out of the forest.
Ich finde den Weg aus dem Wald nicht.
ICH / fin der / dane / Vague / ow!ss / dame / Valt / niCHt.

I am sure we have passed this tree before.
Ich bin sicher, wir sind schon einmal an diesen Baum vorbeigekommen.
ICH / bin / ziCHer, / veer / zint / shone / ine mal / an / dee zen / Bow!m / fir bye geck common.

We will see where we are when the moon comes up.
Wir werden sehen, wo wir sind, wenn der Mond aufgeht.
Veer / vair den / zay yen, / vo / vere / zint, / ven / dare / Moont / ow!f gate.

There are no wolves in Germany, are there?
Es gibt doch keine Wölfe in Deutschland, oder?
Ess / geept / doCH / kye ner / Vurl fur / in / Doy itch lant, / odour?

Let's sing "She'll be coming round the Mountain".
Singen wir "She'll be coming round the Mountain".
Zing gun / veer / "She'll be coming round the Mountain".

At the Beer Festival

Auf dem Bier Fest   Ow!f / dame / Beer / Fest

I'll have a beer, please.
Ich nehme ein Bier, bitte.
Ich / name er / ine / Beer, / bitter.

A small one. *Ein kleines.* **Ine / kly ness.**
A large one. *Ein großes.* **Ine / grocers.**
Another one. *Noch eins.* **NoCH / eye ens.**

I did not expect to pay for the froth on the beer.
*Für den Schaum auf dem Bier wollte ich eigentlich nicht
zahlen.*
**Fewer / dane / Shh ow!m / ow!f / dame / Beer / vol ter /
iCH / eye gunt lick / niCHt / tsar len.**

Which way to the toilets?
Wo geht es zu den Toiletten?
Vo / gate / ess / ts zoo / dane / Toilet ten?

Ine
grocers

50

At the Disco   *In der Diskothek*   In / dare / Disco take

My name is ... What's yours?
Ich heiße ... Wie heißt du?
Icн / high sir ... Vee / heist / doo?

What did you say?
Was hast du gesagt?
Vas / hast / doo / gez sagt?

At the Club   *In der Nachtbar*   In / dare / Naснт bar

For Boys:

Do you come here often?
Kommst du oft hierher?
Kom st / doo / oft / here hair?

Can I buy you a drink?
Darf ich dich zu einem Getränk einladen?
Darf / icн / diсн / ts zoo / eye nem / Get renk / ine lard
den?

Are you on your own?
Bist du allein?
Bist / doo / al line?

Can we get rid of him somehow or other?
Können wir ihn irgendwie loswerden?
Ker nun / veer / een / ear ghent vee / loze vair den?

Give us a kiss.
Gib mir einen Kuss.
Gib / mere / eye nen / Koos.

For girls:

No, I am not alone. I am with – another girl – a man.
Nein, ich bin nicht alleine. Ich bin mit einem anderen Mädchen – mit einem Mann – hier.
Nine, / iCH / bin / nicht / al liner. / ICH / bin / mitt / eye nem – under wren / Maid shen – mitt / eye nem / Mun – here.

The big one with the bald head and tattoos.
Der Große mit der Glatze und den Tätowierungen.
Dare / Grocer / mitt / dare / Glatser / oont / dane / Tet toe veer oon gun.

She fancies you rotten.
Die ist total scharf auf dich.
Dee / ist / total / shh arf / ow!f / diCH.

I think it's a bit too soon for that.
Ich glaube, es ist ein wenig zu früh dafür.
Ich / glow! burr, / ess / ist / ine / vain nig / ts zoo / froo / dah fewer.

Sex *Sex* Sex

Mature female to Toy Boy:

I love that helpless little boy look in your eyes.
Ich liebe diesen hilflosen kleiner-Junge-Blick in deinen Augen.
ICH / lee ber / dee zen / hill floosen / klyner-Yoonger-Blick / in / dine en / Ow! gun.

Do you work out or is that your natural build?
Machst du Bodybuilding oder bist du von Natur aus so gebaut?
MaCH st / doo / Body building / odour / bist / doo / fon / Nah toor / ow!ss / zo / geb out?

Have you finished. So soon?
Bist du schon so schnell fertig?
Bist / doo / shone / zo / shh nell / fair tig?

Sugar Daddy to Nymphette:

Hallo my dear. Can I buy you a cream cake – a beer –
bottle of schnaps?
Hallo meine Liebe. Kann ich dir ein Stück Sahnetorte – ein
Bier – eine Flasche Schnaps kaufen?
Hull law / miner / Lee ber. / Can / iCH / dear / ine / Shh
took / Zarner torter – ine / Beer – eye ner / Flasher / Shh
naps / cow! fen?

Are you on the pill?
Nimmst du die Pille?
Nimst / doo / dee / Pillar?

Won't be a minute. I'll just get my viagra.
Warte eine Minute. Ich hole nur schnell mein Viagra.
Varter / eye ner / Minooter. / ICH / holler / noor / shh nell /
mine / Vee ah grah.

Young Stud to Bimbo:

Are you from around here?
Kommst du hier aus der Gegend?
Komst / doo / hear / ow!ss / dare / Gay ghent?

Like to show me the sights then?
Würdest du mir also gern die Sehenswürdigkeiten zeigen?
Ver dest / doo / mere / alzo / gairn / dee / Zay yens ver
dig kite en / ts eye gun?

All right, darling?
In Ordnung, Schatz?
In / Ord noong, / Shh ats?

53

Sweet Young Thing to Macho Male:

What are you doing?
Was tust du?
Voss / toost / doo?

Leave me alone.
Lass mich in Ruhe.
Lass / miCH / in / Roo er.

I don't fancy you.
Ich mag dich nicht.
ICH / mag / diCH / niCHt.

I have a revolting, pernicious transmitable sexual disease.
Ich habe eine scheußliche, bösartige Geschlechtskrankheit.
ICH / harbour / eye ner / shh oi shh licker, / burrs art tigger / Gay shh leCHts crank height.

The Police   *Die Polizei*   **Dee / Pol its Eye**

The German police are efficient and have been ordered to be tourist friendly, which they are – especially if you have a well-developed figure. If not, when questioned by them, use the following phrase at all times:

I don't understand a thing.
Ich verstehe überhaupt nichts.
ICH / fair shh tayer / oober how! pt / niCHts.

However, if you get into trouble the following may help:

My car has been towed away.
Mein Auto ist weggeschleppt worden.
Mine / Ow! toe / ist / vaguer shh lept / vor den.

I did not see the sign. There was a huge van in the way!
Wie soll ich das Zeichen sehen? Da steht ein verdammter Lieferwagen im Weg!
Vee / zoll / iCH / duss / Tsigh CHen / zay yen? / Da / shh tet / ine / fair dum ter / Leaf air var gun / im / Vague!

My car has been broken into and they have stolen my:
Mein Auto wurde aufgebrochen und man hat mir … gestohlen.
Mine / Ow! toe / vair der / auf ger broCHen / oont / mun / hut / mere / … / guess shh tolen.

Luggage	*das Gepäck*	**duss / Ger peck**
Briefcase	*die Aktentasche*	**dee / Uck ten tasher**
Laptop	*den Laptop*	**dane / Laptop**
Cuckoo clock	*die Kuckucksuhr*	**dee / Cook cooks oo er**

I have been mugged and they have taken my:
Ich bin überfallen worden, und man hat mir … gestohlen:
ICH / bin / oober felon / vorden, / oont / mun / hut / mere / … / guess shh tolen:

Handbag	*die Handtasche*	**dee / Hunt tasher**
Wallet	*die Brieftasche*	**dee / Brief tasher**
Credit cards	*die Kreditkarten*	**dee / Credit carton**
Passport	*der Reisepass*	**dare / Riser pass**
Air ticket	*das Flugticket*	**duss / Floog ticket**

One million in cash.
Eine Million in bar.
Eye ner / Mill yon / in / bar.

Everything I have in the whole wide world.
Alles, was ich auf der ganzen weiten Welt besitze.
Alice, / vass / iCH / ow!f / dare / gunt sen / veye ten / Velt / buzz zits er.

Should you be arrested by mistake, or for inappropriate behaviour, ask for the nearest Consulate (closed at weekends) thus:

I wish to speak to the Ambassador who is a personal friend of mine.
Ich möchte mit dem Botschafter sprechen, der ein persön-licher Freund von mir ist.
ICH / murCH ter / mitt / dame / Boat shaft er / spreCH en, / dare / ine / purse urn liCHer / Froind / fon / mere / ist.

Public Notices You May Come Up Against

GESCHLOSSEN	Closed
GEÖFFNET	Open
SCHLUSSVERKAUF	Sale
INFORMATION	Information
FAHRPLAN	Timetable
FAHRSTUHL	Lift/Elevator
TRINKWASSER	Drinking Water
TOILETTEN	Toilets
DAMEN	Ladies
HERREN	Gentlemen
AUßER BETRIEB	Out of Order
BESETZT	Occupied or Engaged (in a W.C.)
FREI	Vacant/Free
DRÜCKEN	Push/Press
ZIEHEN	Pull

HEBEN	Raise/Lift
KLINGELN	Ring (the bell)
AUSGEBUCHT	No Vacancies
RAUCHEN VERBOTEN	No Smoking
PARKEN VERBOTEN	No Parking
NICHT SPUCKEN	No Spitting
NICHT HERAUSLEHEN	Do Not Lean Out
NICHT BERÜHREN	Do Not Touch
KEIN AUSGANG	No Exit
KEIN EINGANG	No Entry
EINBAHNSTRAßE	One Way Street
FUßGÄNGERÜBERGANG	Pedestrian Crossing
BAHNÜBERGANG	Level Crossing
HALT	Stop
PRIVAT	Private
VERBOTEN	Prohibited
ACHTUNG	Attention
ACHTUNG, BISSIGER HUND	Beware of the dog
GEFAHR	Danger
VOLL	Full

Unlike France and Spain where, confusingly, hot taps are marked with a 'C', in Germany the taps have:

'H' for *Heiß*	Hot
'K' for *Kalt*	Cold

Phrases You May Hear

Vass / voon shun / Zee?
Was wünschen Sie?
What do you want?

Duss / gate / oons / niCHts / an.
Das geht uns nichts an.
That is not our concern.

Zee / moosen / im / Four ow!ss / tsar len.
Sie müssen im Voraus zahlen.
You must pay in advance.

Varter / eye ner / Minooter.
Warte eine Minute.
Wait a minute.

Duss / ist / niCHt / gun oog.
Das ist nicht genug.
That is not enough.

Dee / Bed dee noong / ist / niCHt / im / Price / ine bug griffen.
Die Bedienung ist nicht im Preis einbegriffen.
Service is not included.

Aller / oon searer / Ts simmer – Tisher – zint / buzz sets tt.
Alle unsere Zimmer – Tische – sind besetzt.
All our rooms – tables – are taken.

Zee / kommen / ts zoo / shh pate.
Sie kommen zu spät.
You are too late.

58

Kommen / Zee / shh pay ter / veeder.
Kommen Sie später wieder.
Come back later.

Vuss / muCHen / Zee?
Was machen Sie?
What are you doing?

Duss / ist / niCHt / air low!bt.
Das ist nicht erlaubt.
That is not allowed.

Ear wren / Narmen / bitter.
Ihren Namen, bitte.
Your name, please.

Vair / ist / dran?
Wer ist dran?
Who is next?

Vel CHes / Shh tock verk / vol learn / Zee?
Welches Stockwerk wollen Sie?
Which floor do you want?

Zee / har ben / dee / false sher / Nummer.
Sie haben die falsche Nummer.
You have the wrong number.

ICH / vice / ess / niCHt.
Ich weiß es nicht.
I don't know.

Frah gun / Zee / miCH / niCHt, / iCH / bin / hear / zelb st / fremt.
Fragen Sie mich nicht, ich bin hier selbst fremd.
Don't ask me, I'm a stranger here myself.

Last Words

I miss you.
Ich vermisse Dich.
ICH / fair miss sir / DICH.

See you. *Bis bald.* **Biss / bahlt.**

Please say that again, but more slowly.
Sag das bitte noch einmal, aber langsamer.
Zag / duss / bitter / noCH / ine mal, / arbour / lung ts armour.

Is there anyone here who speaks English?
Gibt es hier irgendjemanden, der Englisch spricht?
Geept / ess / hear / ear ghent yay munden, / dare / En glish / spricHt?

Biss bahlt

60